Powered by: youthministry360 + LeaderTreks.

This Book Belongs To:

Date:

the **pause.**
learning to seek God

Published by youth**ministry**360 in the United States of America.

ISBN 13: 978 1 935832 140
ISBN 10: 1 935832 14 0

Author: Andy Blanks
Design: Upper Air Creative
Copy Editor: Lynn Groom

I SEEK YOU WITH ALL MY HEART; DO NOT LET ME STRAY FROM YOUR COMMANDS. I HAVE HIDDEN YOUR WORD IN MY HEART THAT I MIGHT NOT SIN AGAINST YOU.

—PSALM 119:10-11

CONTENTS

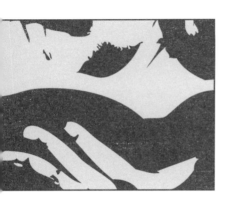

GETTING STARTED ...

IF YOU'RE HOLDING THIS BOOK RIGHT NOW, THERE'S A GOOD CHANCE YOU HAVE, AT SOME TIME IN THE RECENT PAST, SPENT A FAIR AMOUNT OF TIME STUDYING WHAT IT MEANS TO "HIT PAUSE."*

MAYBE YOU STUDIED THE PAUSE AS PART OF A DISCIPLE NOW WEEKEND, OR A WEEKEND RETREAT.

Maybe you did it in your small group, or on Wednesday nights.

Whatever the case, there was a moment when you reached the last session and you "finished" your look at the why's and how's of hitting pause. Or so you thought.

THIS BOOK YOU'RE HOLDING REPRESENTS THE NEXT PHASE OF YOUR JOURNEY.

In this book, you're going to take a much deeper look at this concept. And you're going to do it in a way that's a little different. For most of you this means no small group, no leader. Just you, this book, your Bible, and the Holy Spirit as your guide.

The weekend you might have spent studying *The Pause* with your youth group was really only the beginning. This next stage of the journey is where you'll have the chance to go so much deeper in how you learn to hit pause and what a commitment to knowing God can do for your life. And that's pretty exciting stuff . . .

LET'S GET STARTED. READ THE NEXT PAGE TO LEARN EXACTLY HOW THIS BOOK WORKS.

*Technically, you don't HAVE to have gone through *The Pause* with your group. But, you'll probably get a lot more out of this book if you have.

HOW THIS BOOK WORKS

Here are a few things you need to know to put this book to good use.

Start With This Advice

Whether you're super-committed and read your Bible each day, or struggle to read a few verses a couple of times a week, the key to sticking with this through four weeks is a routine. Try to work through this book the same time each day, whether that's in the morning, after lunch, or before you go to bed. Block out a time each day to spend in this book, and then commit to sticking to it. **You'll find it's a lot easier to stay consistent that way.**

Have Your Bible Open

Resist the urge to ignore the spots where this book will tell you to read a passage of Scripture. This book is only a guide for THE Book. **The close relationship with God that you want only happens by reading and doing what's in the Bible.** Have it open as you go through this book.

Each Week Is Structured The Same, But Is Really Different

Each week's content follows a pattern. **But each day is different. And there are a lot of different kinds of activities.** Some will take 3-5 minutes, some 10-15. Some will ask you to look at two or three passages of Scripture, some will just ask you to think about a concept. The variety will make it easier to stick with, and will help you learn in different ways that are suited to you.

What If I Miss A Day of Reading? Or Three?

Don't give up! Take this at your pace! The goal is for you to grow closer to God and to have a faith-life that's more "real"! If you miss a day or two . . . or four . . . don't throw in the towel. Pick this book back up and start where you left off. **You can do this!** And by doing it, you'll show the world that God makes an incredible difference in the lives of His followers. So, hang in there! You've got this!

WELL, THAT'S WHAT YOU NEED TO KNOW TO GET STARTED! TURN THE PAGE TO READ THE INTRODUCTION TO WEEK 1.

WEEK 1: INTRO

BEFORE STARTING WEEK 1, READ THIS SHORT INTRODUCTION.

Have you ever had a moment where you learned something about a friend that really took you by surprise?

> Maybe it was a super-awesome "hidden" talent, such as barrel racing, or jiujitsu.

> Maybe it was something sad, such as the loss of a sibling earlier in life.

> Or maybe it was something weird. "Oh . . . Well, look at that . . . You *do* have six toes . . ."

Whatever it is, the moment you realize there's more to a person you thought you knew pretty well already--well, it's kind of cool. You realize how deep people really are.

TAKE THIS PRINCIPLE AND MULTIPLY IT TIMES INFINITY, AND YOU HAVE A SLIGHT GRASP OF WHAT IT MEANS TO KNOW, AND TO GET TO KNOW GOD.

At its very core, the idea of "hitting pause" is all about relationship. It's all about getting to know God. And while we'll never fully know Him this side of eternity, it's His plan that we seek to know Him. Over the course of the next four weeks, we'll do just that.

But we'll start Week 1 with a little review of what you know (and maybe some of what you forgot) about The Pause.

So, let's get started! Turn to page 5 for Week 1, Day 1.

Those who know your name
will trust in you, for you,
LORD, have never forsaken
those who seek you.
—**Psalm 9:10**

cs

WEEK 1: DAY 1

Today's content is a quick review of what you should have covered in *The Pause.*
Read the following verses, and then follow with the questions to recall anything you learned, or simply to begin reflecting again on these concepts.

Pause CONCEPT 1
Seeking God through prayer and Bible Study is vital to your faith.

Read This: Very early in the morning, while it was still dark, Jesus got up, left the house and went off to a solitary place, where he prayed. —Mark 1:35

Now, answer this question in the space provided:
   • How often do you intentionally set aside time in your schedule to spend with God--just you and Him?

I feel horrible. about this, but Never.

Pause CONCEPT 2
Prayer is the language of our relationship with God.
No prayer = poor relationship.

Read This: Pray continually.—1 Thessalonians 5:17

Now, answer these questions in the space provided:
   • Describe the state of your prayer life. Healthy? Unhealthy but alive? On life support? Or dead?
   • How does this make you feel?

On life Support
Like I'm going to Hell

Pause CONCEPT 3
It's impossible to be in relationship with God without studying the Bible.

Read This: I will study your commandments and reflect on your ways. I will delight in your decrees and not forget your word.—Psalm 119:15-16 (NLT)

Now, answer these questions in the space provided:
- What is your attitude toward the Bible?
- Can you honestly say you delight in it?

I think it gets boring but when I get into it I can absolutely feel God's presence.

Pause CONCEPT 4
Hitting pause prepares you to live out your purpose. Your purpose = drawing others to God.

Read This: We are therefore Christ's ambassadors, as though God were making his appeal through us. We implore you on Christ's behalf: Be reconciled to God.—2 Corinthians 5:20

Now, answer this question in the space provided:
- In your words, what is an "ambassador"?
- Can you think of a few ways in the last weeks or months that you've acted as an ambassador for Christ?

- Someone who has a lot of power

Alright! Now that you're back in the flow, you should remember these concepts. It's a good foundation for starting this book. But tomorrow's activity is a lot different, so don't miss it!

WEEK 1: DAY 2

Remember, we're in review mode for the next few days. To make sure we're on the same page, let's define what we mean when we talk about hitting pause.

TO HIT PAUSE IS TO . . .

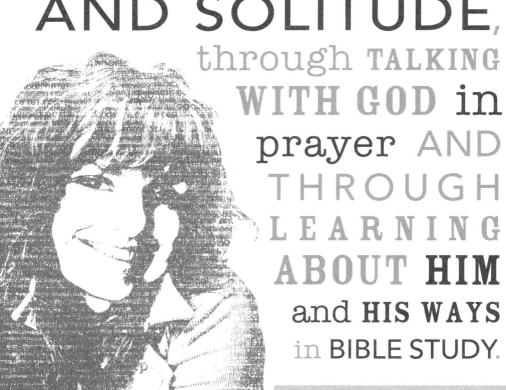

...SEEK GOD in silence AND SOLITUDE, through TALKING WITH GOD in prayer AND THROUGH LEARNING ABOUT **HIM** and **HIS WAYS** in BIBLE STUDY.

Let's dig in to this definition a little bit. Don't rush this: if you grasp this concept, it will push you to learn how to be more effective at hitting pause.

1. The key parts of hitting pause were set apart in the definition. Write them in the space provided below.

   - seek god in SILENCE
   - talk to god with prayer
   - learn about god in bible study

2. What does seeking God in silence look like in your world? Start by thinking about this: What in your life creates "noise" or distracts you?

   The things ~~that~~ in my life that distract me are electronics, friends, my dog, food...

3. Solitude. Sounds serious! But what does it really mean? And why is it important?

   Solitude is being alone, it is important because if we aren't alone with God we probably wouldn't be truly in his presence.

4. In the definition, prayer and Bible Study are mentioned. Why both? How would your prayers be affected if you couldn't know God through the Bible? And how would reading the Bible be affected by not being able to talk and listen to God?

   If you didn't read the bible it could make you think that you know God but really not be connecting when you pray!

AS YOU GO THROUGHOUT YOUR DAY, OR AS YOU GET READY FOR BED, THINK ABOUT HOW YOU CAN APPLY THESE CONCEPTS IN YOUR LIFE. **SEE YOU TOMORROW ON WEEK 1, DAY 3.**

WEEK 1: DAY 3

How de we see the idea of hitting pause play out in the Bible? Here are just a few examples. Read the passages. Then on pg.10, using the definition of hitting pause you looked at yesterday, jot down how you see the idea of hitting pause showing up in these passages.

Read Daniel 6:10

Now when Daniel learned that the decree had been published, he went home to his upstairs room where the windows opened toward Jerusalem. Three times a day he got down on his knees and prayed, giving thanks to his God, just as he had done before.

Read 1 Samuel 3:19-21

The LORD was with Samuel as he grew up, and he let none of his words fall to the ground. And all Israel from Dan to Beersheba recognized that Samuel was attested as a prophet of the LORD. The LORD continued to appear at Shiloh, and there he revealed himself to Samuel through his word.

Read Psalm 63:1

[A psalm of David. When he was in the Desert of Judah.]
O God, you are my God, earnestly I seek you; my soul thirsts for you, my body longs for you, in a dry and weary land where there is no water.

How do you see Daniel practicing some aspect of hitting pause?

Daniel went to his upstairs and prayed three times a day... just him and God.

Here we see the result of Samuel having committed to hitting pause in his life. What was the result?

The result was that all of Israel knew Samuel as a phrophet of the LORD.

How do David's words here relate to what we talked about in defining the pause yesterday?

When David says "in a dry and weary land where there is no water." I think he's referring to being alone with no one else discussing any problems in his life.

Knowing that others have practiced hitting pause to seek God is important. It shows us that we're simply doing what people have done for thousands of years to draw close to God. Let's keep a good thing going!

WEEK 1: DAY 4

Today you're going to practice two aspects of hitting pause.

Today, take 15 minutes to be completely by yourself. **Find solitude.** And Find someplace quiet to do it. **Find silence.** Don't answer your phone or text messages. **Be alone.** Listen to the silence of your surroundings. If you feel led, talk to Him in prayer. And listen for Him to talk back.

"THE CHRISTIAN MUST FIGHT TO BE ALONE WITH GOD AND TO KEEP TIME FOR KNOWING GOD."
— DONALD GREY BARNHOUSE*

Thoughts to consider:

- How well can you relate to this? *It's hard*

- Does it seem at times (or all the time) that you have to fight for time to seek God? *Yes, a lot of the time*

- What are the biggest obstacles or issues that compete with God for your time? *School, homework, friends*

- Think about that last question. Should anything really have to compete with God for your time? *No, I feel guilty about it*

- Why does it take time to know God? *Because you have to be committed*

- Why do you even care? Why is it important to you to know God? Or is it not? What do your actions say about how important it is to you? *I KNOW it is important but my actions say I don't even care*

WEEK 1: DAY 6

Read the following devotion and answer the questions at the end.

Read Matthew 14:15-24.

Seven times in the Gospels, the word *alone* is used in relation to Jesus. In two other occasions, Jesus is described as being "by Himself." In yet another instance Jesus is said to have "withdrawn . . . to a solitary place." And in one account we see Him apparently praying by Himself when the disciples burst in to ask if He would teach them to pray!

From reading the Gospels, it's obvious that Jesus understood the importance of looking for quiet time alone to be in relationship with God. In each of these instances, Jesus is pictured as being all by Himself. And in each of them the point seems to be that Jesus was either praying or otherwise communicating with God.

"Uh, isn't Jesus God?" you might ask. "Couldn't He be in relationship with God whenever He wanted?" It's a very interesting question. (Bonus points if you were already thinking this way.) The answer is probably something like this: Jesus was fully God and fully man. We can't know the ins and outs of all this meant to His relationship with God, the Father. But we do know this: the people who wrote the Gospels either saw or talked to people who saw Jesus going away, by Himself, to pray and communicate with God. So, it was obviously important for Jesus. **And if was important for Jesus, it must be important for us.**

- Think back on Week 1, Day 4 when you made time to be alone and in silence. What was that like? Was it nice to set aside time to spend talking and listening to God? *Yes, but because I'm not use to it, it was a little bit before I didn't feel weird.*
- If you didn't take time to do it, why not? What are you waiting on? Isn't it time you stopped letting life get in the way of your relationship with God? If you need to go back to page 11 and follow what it says. **It's worth it.**

WEEK 1: DAY 7

REVIEW AND REFLECT

You've covered a lot this week. Thumb back through the pages and re-member what you learned. Consider this: Are you putting what you're learning to work in your life? **As you get ready for bed, or get ready to start your day, think about some of the more meaningful things you learned this week.** And get ready for next week. It's going to be awesome.

WEEK 1: WRAPPING UP

Review time is over! Hopefully you learned something new in Week 1 and were able to put it to use. That's kind of a big deal, the whole "putting it to use" thing. I mean, let's face it: if you're not actually doing the stuff we've been talking about, you're missing it. **A relationship with God is life-changing.** But you have to put the principles in place to see it grow.

If you're ready to get serious about growing closer to God, you're in the right place. The rest of this journal is going to really take you deeper into what it means to hit pause. Get ready! If you put yourself in a position to accept what you learn, your life could be transformed pretty dramatically.

THE PAUSE EXTRA: #1

The Bible has a lot to say about seeking God in order to grow closer to Him. After all, that's what hitting pause is all about, right? As you have time, read these verses and soak in what it means to grow closer to God.

MY SOUL FINDS REST IN GOD ALONE; MY SALVATION COMES FROM HIM. PSALM 62:1

I HAVE TOLD YOU THESE THINGS, SO THAT IN ME YOU MAY HAVE PEACE. IN THIS WORLD YOU WILL HAVE TROUBLE. BUT TAKE HEART! I HAVE OVERCOME THE WORLD. — JOHN 16:33

In the same way, let your light shine before men, that they may see your good deeds and praise your Father in heaven.— Matthew 5:16

Come to me, all you who are weary and burdened, and I will give you rest. Take my yoke upon you and learn from me, for I am gentle and humble in heart, and you will find rest for your souls. For my yoke is easy and my burden is light.—Matthew 11:28-30

YOU WILL SEEK ME AND FIND ME WHEN YOU SEEK ME WITH ALL YOUR HEART.—JEREMIAH 29:13

COME NEAR TO GOD AND HE WILL COME NEAR TO YOU.—JAMES 4:8

For the LORD watches over the way of the righteous, but the way of the wicked will perish.—Psalm 1:6

But seek first his kingdom and his righteousness, and all these things will be given to you as well.—Matthew 6:33

IF YOU REMAIN IN ME AND MY WORDS REMAIN IN YOU, ASK WHATEVER YOU WISH, AND IT WILL BE GIVEN YOU.—JOHN 15:7

20

WEEK 2: INTRO

BEFORE STARTING WEEK 2, READ THIS SHORT INTRODUCTION

Take a moment and picture whomever it is that's primarily responsible for your care. Got 'em pictured in your mind? Good.

Now, picture the following three scenarios.

Scenario One: You live with this person day after day. But you have no communication with him or her at all. Zero. No notes. No texts. No conversation. Nothing!

Scenario Two: Same person, same arrangement. But, there's some communication. A text here, a quick conversation there. Not a lot of communication. But some.

Scenario Three: Picture your current life with your parent or guardian. You can communicate. You can talk. You can text. You can get on the same page.

Which one of these scenarios would you rather have? Of course it's scenario three. Scenario one is impossible. Can you imagine what this would be like? How would you ever know anything? How would you get anything accomplished? Scenario two would be an improvement, but not by much. Scenario three works because, well, because that's how it's intended to work.

COMMUNICATION MAKES RELATIONSHIPS WORK.

Where does your relationship with God fall on this spectrum of communication? Are you like the first scenario, never communicating? Do you talk some? Or have you jumped on board with God through a deep and meaningful line of open communication?

PRAYER IS AT THE HEART OF OUR COMMUNICATION WITH GOD. IT IS AT THE HEART OF HITTING PAUSE. AND THIS WEEK, WEEK 2, IS ALL ABOUT PRAYER.

Get ready. It's going to be awesome.

But I pray to you, O LORD, in the time of your favor; in your great love, O God, answer me with your sure salvation.—**Psalm 69:13**

WEEK 2: DAY 1

Now seems like the perfect time to think about how you think about prayer.
(That's a lot of thinking. You "think" you can handle it?)

CLEAR YOUR MIND FOR A SECOND AND REALLY THINK ABOUT THE ANSWER TO THIS QUESTION: WHAT IS YOUR ATTITUDE TOWARD PRAYER?

Do you enjoy praying?
Does it bore you?
Do you do it because you want to?
Do you do it because you have to?
Do you not do it at all?
Do you feel like you know how?
Or do you feel lost?
Do you get distracted?
Do you love talking to God?
Do you listen?
Does prayer make God feel more real?
Do you thank God?
Or just ask for stuff?
Do you pray when you're scared?
Do you pray when you're happy?
Do you pray when things are going really, really well?
Do you miss God when you go too long without praying?
Is it hard to remember the last time you prayed?

"Do not be anxious about anything, but in everything, by prayer and petition, with thanksgiving, present your requests to God." Philippians 4:6

PRAYER IS IMPORTANT.

Prayer is vital to your relationship with God. You can't know God unless you get to know Him. If you need to reevaluate your attitude toward prayer, now's a great time to do it. If you are a Christ-follower, prayer should be second nature.

PRAYER IS YOUR PIPELINE TO GOD. PLAIN AND SIMPLE.

WEEK 2: DAY 2

Did you know there are different kinds of prayers? Read the verses below and interact with the questions to discover some of the ways we talk to God in prayer.

HAVE YOU EVER ASKED GOD FOR SOMETHING?

Of course you have! In fact, for most people this is the most common type of prayer. *People who like using big words call this type of prayer supplication.*

Read these passages to see where this type of prayer pops up in the Bible:
- Luke 11:9-13
- 1 John 5:14

HAVE YOU EVER PRAYED FOR SOMEONE ELSE?

Sure you have! You've probably even prayed for something on someone else's behalf. *Our friends who love the big words call this type of prayer intercession.*

Read these passages to see where this type of prayer pops up in the Bible:
- Acts 12:1-5
- John 17:13-19

HAVE YOU EVER PRAYED TO GOD AND TALKED TO HIM ABOUT YOUR SINS?

The answer is most definitely yes. And this prayer is usually accompanied by a plea for forgiveness. *Remember our friends who like big words? They call this prayer* confession. *I've heard of before!!*

Read these passages to see where this type of prayer pops up in the Bible:
- Psalm 51:1-6
- 1 John 1:9

HAVE YOU EVER THANKED GOD FOR WHAT HE'S DONE FOR YOU?

If you haven't, we need to talk. Seriously, though. Hopefully this is a pretty common prayer of yours. *Our big word-liking friends must have run out of words because this type of prayer is simply called a prayer of* thanksgiving.

Read these passages to see where this type of prayer pops up in the Bible:
- Psalm 100
- 1 Thessalonians 5:16-18

SOMETHING TO THINK ABOUT:
- How does it help you to know some of the main types of prayers you find in the Bible?
- How can you use these categories of prayers to bring focus to your prayer life?
- Did you see a category of prayer that you don't really practice that much? What if you were to focus more on praying this type of prayer for a few days? How do you think that would help grow your understanding of God and how He relates to us?

WEEK 2: DAY 3

Prayer was important to Jesus. So much so that after observing Him pray, His disciples asked Him to teach them how to pray. His response gives us a model for how to pray to God.

Open your Bible to Matthew 6:9-13.

You may remember this from studying *The Pause* with your group. But by looking at the Lord's Prayer, we can see some guidelines for our prayers. Read the verses below, look at their corresponding guidelines, and consider the questions after each one.

Praise God
Read Matthew 6:9

Here Jesus is teaching us that praising God is vitally important to our prayer life.

- What are some things you normally praise God for?

- How does praising God deepen your relationship with Him?

Open My Eyes
Read Matthew 6:10

Jesus is helping us be aware of God's will and His rule over all things. We pray that we can be a part of God's will being done on this earth.

- What are some practical ways your life is a part of God's plan to bring people in relationship with Him?

Ask The Father
Read Matthew 6:11

Jesus shows us that asking God to meet our needs, and trusting Him to follow through, is an important part of prayer.

- What are the differences between needs and wants?

- Why does God sometimes not answer our prayers like we want Him to? How can this sometimes relate to a need versus a want?

Seek and Give Mercy
Read Matthew 6:12

We sin. We sin against God and against others. And other people sin against us, too. Jesus is helping us to pray for forgiveness, and to offer it to others.

- Forgiveness is a pretty cool thing. When was the last time you thought about how amazing it is that God forgives us through Christ?

- When you show forgiveness to others, how are you identifying yourself with God and His ways?

Give Me Strength
Read Matthew 6:13

Jesus knows that our sin keeps us from being as close to God as we could be. So, He teaches us to pray for the strength to overcome it.

- How aware are you of the sin in your life that really trips you up? How might you pray specifically that God would help you deal with that sin?

WEEK 2: DAY 4

Today you're going to practice an aspect of the pause.

The length of your prayers doesn't matter to God. But, for many of us, we aren't in the practice of making time to pray. So, today, think about how long you normally pray. **Then double it.** Set aside time to be by yourself with no distractions and pray to God. If you want, use the different categories of prayer from pages 25 and 26 as your guide. **Praise God. Thank God. Pray for others.** Confess your sins. Then bring your needs to God, trusting Him to meet them according to His will.

WEEK 2: DAY 5

Read this quote. Then, take some time to reflect on it.

"BECAUSE GOD IS THE LIVING GOD, HE CAN HEAR; BECAUSE HE IS A LOVING GOD, HE WILL HEAR; BECAUSE HE IS OUR COVENANT GOD, HE HAS BOUND HIMSELF TO HEAR."*—C. H. SPURGEON

Thoughts to consider:

- What does it mean that God is the living God? If God were not living and active in His creation, how would that affect our prayers?

- How does God reveal through our prayers that He is truly alive and that He does hear us?

- What if you had to earn God's love in order for Him to listen to and answer our prayers? How would that change everything?

- What impact does God's unconditional and unfailing love have on the way we pray and think about prayer?

- Remember, when Spurgeon talks about the idea of a "covenant," he is referring to God's eternal commitment to be perfectly faithful to the relationship He has with all who believe in Him. How does God's faithfulness to His relationship with you change the way you pray to Him?

WEEK 2: DAY 6

Read the following devotion and answer the questions at the end.

Do you ever have one of those days? Those moments in life where you know you want to pray to God, but you don't know what to say?

Maybe you're going through a seriously hard time.
Maybe you just feel distant from God.
Maybe you have an issue you don't know what to do about.

Whatever the case, there are times when we can't seem to put what we want into words. What do you do in these times? Here's some hope for you.

Read Romans 8:26-27.

Now, this language can be a bit confusing. But let's look at it. Paul is telling the Roman Christ-followers that when they are weak, hurt, and lost, there is a Helper that comes alongside them. Remember the concept of "intercession" we talked about on page 25? How cool is it that the Holy Spirit intercedes for us? The Holy Spirit literally takes our needs before God. And God hears the "groanings" of the Spirit and will meet our needs according to His will.

Whoa! Now that's absolutely amazing. How cool is it that when you're at your lowest and don't know how or what to pray to God, the Holy Spirit steps in and takes over. It's a powerful thing. **And one that can give us great hope and comfort.**

- Has there ever been a time when you weren't sure how to pray? Or were hurting in a way that you couldn't really pray?

  Yes

- What does it make you feel like knowing that in that time of your life, the Holy Spirit was on your side, bringing your needs to God?

  I feel wonderful and amazed.

WEEK 2: DAY 7

REVIEW AND REFLECT

Reflect back and think about times you experienced God's presence this week. Or maybe times you didn't. Think about a way you prayed this week that might have been different from how you've prayed before. Reflect on how focusing on prayer this week changed your heart. And then think about what you might do moving forward to help make this newfound emphasis on prayer a part of your life.

REFLECT

WEEK 2: WRAPPING UP

Do you feel like you have a better idea of how prayer works as a critical part of your relationship with God? Good. Because, you know . . . It's important. Really important. But hopefully after spending all this time focusing on it, you get that. Having a healthy prayer life is a major part of having a healthy relationship with God. **But it's not the only part.**

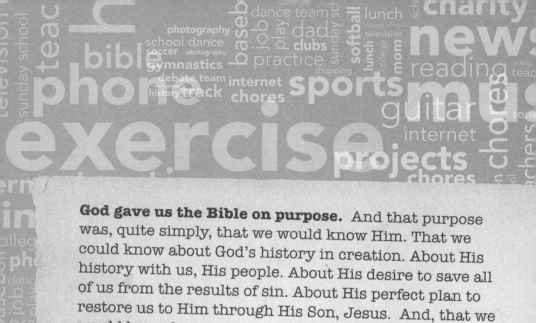

God gave us the Bible on purpose. And that purpose was, quite simply, that we would know Him. That we could know about God's history in creation. About His history with us, His people. About His desire to save all of us from the results of sin. About His perfect plan to restore us to Him through His Son, Jesus. And, that we would know how to live as His children. All of this is in the Bible. But if you don't study it, you won't know it. That's what next week is all about. **Get ready, because you're about to dig in to God's Word.**

THE PAUSE EXTRA: #2

"WHY DIDN'T GOD ANSWER MY PRAYER?"

Well, the Bible says over and over again that God does, in fact, answer our prayers.

O you who hear prayer, to you all men will come.—Psalm 65:2
I call on you, O God, for you will answer me; give ear to me and hear my prayer.—Psalm 17:6

So if you know this, and you still believe God didn't answer your prayer, what could the explanation be? Let's look at some possibilities.

Possibility 1: God didn't answer your prayer because what you were praying for wasn't inline with God's character and/or plan.

The eyes of the LORD are on the righteous and his ears are attentive to their cry.—Psalm 34:15
The LORD is far from the wicked but he hears the prayer of the righteous.—Proverbs 15:29

God will answer prayers that come from the heart of someone who has God's ways and will in mind. In other words, a righteous person--a child of God. If answering what you're asking would cause God to act against His character, God won't answer your prayer. Our prayers must be godly prayers, in line with His will.

Possibility 2: God didn't answer your prayer in exactly the way you wanted Him to, but He did answer it.

"Which of you, if his son asks for bread, will give him a stone? Or if he asks for a fish, will give him a snake? If you, then, though you are evil, know how to give good gifts to your children, how much more will your Father in heaven give good gifts to those who ask him!"—Matthew 7:9-11

Because God is all-powerful and all-knowing, He knows what you need. And He knows the best way to answer you. God will answer your prayers in ways that bring gory to Him and are the best outcome for you according to His will. It might not be the way you expect, but He will answer your prayers.

Possibility 3: God's answer isn't obvious today, but it may be one day.

> "Do not be like them, for your Father knows what you need before you ask him."—Matthew 6:8

God knows what you need. And sometimes, He gives it to you in a way and in a timing that might not be apparent to you. Many times, you can only see why God worked the way He did when you're able to look back after time has passed.

Possibility 4: You may never know why God chose to respond to your prayer the way He did.

This is especially true when it comes to death, sickness, and loss. When you prayed for your parent or sibling's cancer to be healed, and it wasn't, how is that God answering your prayer? This is for many people the single most challenging aspect of their relationship with God. We can't know exactly why God works the way He does:

> "For my thoughts are not your thoughts, neither are your ways my ways," declares the LORD. As the heavens are higher than the earth, so are my ways higher than your ways and my thoughts than your thoughts."—Isaiah 55:8-9

We can't know why God allows bad things to happen to good people. And in these moments, we may feel like God doesn't answer our prayers. But we have to know that God is good and only plans good for us:

> And we know that in all things God works for the good of those who love him, who have been called according to his purpose.—Romans 8:28

Therefore, we have to trust that God will bring all things to pass according to His plan, and in line with His character. This is where trust comes in. If we trust God to be God when things go well for us, we have to trust Him when things aren't going well.

> Those who know your name will trust in you, for you, LORD, have never forsaken those who seek you.—Psalm 9:10

WEEK 3: INTRO

This week you're going to be focusing your attention on the Bible.

When you read that sentence, what did you feel? Boredom? Excitement? Nervousness? Guilt? Joy? Or, did you feel nothing?

The concept of "knowing the Bible" gets a bad wrap, sometimes. But it's not the Bible's fault. And it's certainly not God's fault.

People may be intimidated or apathetic toward the Bible for a few reasons. But mostly, it seems like it's because they either don't know what to do with it, or they don't understand how important it is to their relationship with God.

If you studied *The Pause* with your group, you learned a little of how to study the Bible. You know what to do with it, and you're going to learn some more this week. But what about the importance of the Bible?

Without the Bible, what do you have as the basis of your relationship with God?

Experience is unreliable and potentially misleading.

EMOTIONS ARE FLEETING. JUST BECAUSE YOU DON'T FEEL GOD DOESN'T MEAN HE ISN'T THERE.

Other people can teach you about God, but how do you know if what they're teaching is right without the Bible?

The truth is, the Bible is God's plan for you to get to know Him. So, let's spend the next few days really looking at the Bible and how we interact with it.

For the
active
sword
soul and
judges
the heart

WEEK 3: DAY 1

If you studied *The Pause* with your group, this may look familiar.
But in case you didn't, or in case you lost your Pause Student Book, here is a review of exactly HOW to study a passage of Scripture.

Meditating on God's Word

If you recall, there are two ways to interact with the Bible: meditating and mining. Let's look at meditating first. Remember, in Psalm 1, David described a blessed man by saying:

> *His delight is in the law of the LORD, and on his law he meditates day and night.*

If you recall, meditating on God's Word is simple. Basically you read it and think about it. (Told you it was simple.) **So how do you do it?**

STEP 1: Choose a passage. (duh)

STEP 2: Clear your thoughts and pray that the Holy Spirit will help you see God's truth in this passage. Read the passage.

STEP 3: Read the passage again, thinking about what each word is saying.

STEP 4: Clear your head of any distractions. Now read the verses one last time, focusing on words that jump out at you. You may choose to circle these words or phrases, or write them in a journal.

Then, ask yourself these questions:

- How do these verses make you feel?

- What do you want to say to God after reading this?

- How might these verses change your outlook on your day or your life?

That's pretty much it. That's all there is to meditating on God's Word.

Mining God's Word

Meditating on God's Word is important. But mining is, too. If you recall, mining is searching the depths of God's Word for a greater understanding of specific passages.

STEP 1: Again, choose a passage.

STEP 2: Read the passage. Read it again, paying attention to what stands out as important.

STEP 3: Write down your thoughts. Circle any words you don't know. Ask questions. For anything that looks significant, write it down.

> **NOTE:** If you have questions, now is the time to answer them. How? Here are few thoughts:
>
> - Buy a Bible Dictionary or a Study Bible. These help.
> - Search for key words in the concordance in the back of your Bible.
> - Ask your parents, youth worker, or another adult you trust.

STEP 4: Know the context.
- Go back a few verses before the passage you're studying. Read until you come to your passage.

- Now read a few verses past your passage. You should have a better idea of what's going on now.

STEP 5: Find the main idea. Write down what you think the main truth of the passage is.

STEP 6: Live the truth. The Bible must influence your life. Live out the main truth of this passage today.

YOU NOW HAVE THE TOOLS TO DO TWO DIFFERENT KINDS OF BIBLE STUDIES. WHAT ARE YOU WAITING FOR? CHOOSE A PASSAGE OF SCRIPTURE AND PUT WHAT YOU KNOW TO USE.

WEEK 3: DAY 2

Read this quote. Then, take some time to reflect on it.

"THE WORD OF THE LORD IS A LIGHT TO GUIDE YOU, A COUNSELOR TO COUNSEL YOU, A COMFORTER TO COMFORT YOU, A STAFF TO SUPPORT YOU, A SWORD TO DEFEND YOU, AND A PHYSICIAN TO CURE YOU. THE WORD IS A MINE TO ENRICH YOU, A ROBE TO CLOTHE YOU, AND A CROWN TO CROWN YOU."
—THOMAS BROOKS

Thoughts to consider:

- This quote speaks to many of the different ways the Bible works in our lives. Are there a few roles in this quote that you can relate to?

- What are some specific times in your life that God's Word has made an impact in your life?

- Is there a role the Bible plays in your life that's not reflected in this quote?

- In what ways can the Bible comfort and support you?

- How is the Bible a sword to defend you?

- If you're honest, did you have trouble relating to any of these thoughts because the Bible simply doesn't have a place in your life? Are you OK with this? Or are you willing to change your habits?

WEEK 3: DAY 3

Today, your only task is to set aside 10-15 minutes of time to study God's Word. Choose one of the two methods of studying God's Word demonstrated on pages 41 and 42. Choose a few verses of Scripture, and spend some time really studying God's Word. Then, focus on how the truths you learn stick with you the rest of the day. **Don't miss this chance to learn more about God and how His Word impacts your life.**

WEEK 3: DAY 4

Do you keep God's Word with you all day? Read the verse below, and then see how you'll answer the challenge on the next page.

For too many people, it's enough to simply read their Bible once a day. In fact, we tend to think of these folks as the ones who have it together. But the Bible doesn't draw the line at the "once a day" approach. The Bible seems to imply that we keep God's Word with us all day, all the time. See for yourself:

The law of his God is in his heart; his feet do not slip.—Psalm 37:31

Oh, how I love your law! I meditate on it all day long.—Psalm 119:97

"These commandments that I give you today are to be upon your hearts. Impress them on your children. Talk about them when you sit at home and when you walk along the road, when you lie down and when you get up. Tie them as symbols on your hands and bind them on your foreheads. Write them on the doorframes of your houses and on your gates."
—Deuteronomy 6:6-9

So how do you do this? How do you keep God's Word in your heart? How do you meditate on God's Word all day? How do you talk about the Word at home and on the road? These questions should get you thinking . . .

SO, HOW DO YOU DO THIS? HOW DO YOU BREAK THROUGH THE HABIT OF THINKING THAT THE BIBLE IS JUST FOR YOUR QUIET TIME AND NOT FOR THE REST OF YOUR LIFE? HERE ARE A FEW THOUGHTS:

Paper Is Your Friend

Keep a few slips of paper in your pocket with Bible verses written on them. Pull them out and look at them throughout the day.

Embrace Technology

Use a Bible app on your smart phone. Read a verse or two between classes. Or after lunch. Or before practice. Or on the way home.

Embrace Technology, Part 2

There are some really awesome audio Bible translations out there. They range from plain ones with just one person reading the text to pretty cool ones with sound effects and music. If you think you'd benefit from listening to the Bible on your phone or MP3 player, ask your parents to buy you one of the many, great audio Bible apps.

Go Portable

You know, you can bring your Bible to school with you. It doesn't turn to dust when it leaves your bedroom. What if you made time between a class or before or after lunch to read a few verses, and simply use them to keep you close to God during the day? You might find your relationship with God will deepen more than you expect.

WHAT DO YOU DO TO KEEP GOD'S WORD IN YOUR HEART?

WEEK 3: DAY 5

How do you feel about God's Word? Read the passage below and interact with the questions on page 50.

7 The **LAW** of the LORD is perfect,
   reviving the soul.
   The **STATUTES** of the LORD are trustworthy,
   making wise the simple.
8 The **PRECEPTS** of the LORD are right,
   giving joy to the heart.
   The **COMMANDS** of the LORD are radiant,
   giving light to the eyes.
9 The fear of the LORD is pure,
   enduring forever.
   The **ORDINANCES** of the LORD are sure
   and altogether righteous.
10 They are more precious than gold,
   than much pure gold;
   they are sweeter than honey,
   than honey from the comb.
11 By them is your servant warned;
   in keeping them there is great reward.
                              —Psalm 19:7-11

The bold words you see in the passage on page 49 all refer to God's commands, or His teachings. These are the parts of Scripture that directly relate to how we are to live our lives. Now, look at how the psalmist described these words.

Circle the words that are used to describe God's Word.

Now, go one step forward. **Underline every place in this passage that speaks to how God's Word makes us feel, or brings a benefit to us.**

Done? Now, ask yourself this question: How does God's Word make you feel? **Can you write down three phrases that describe how you feel when you interact with God's Word?**

1. Connected, want to do right thing

2. Loyal, loving

3. Refreshed, amazing

Of the four phrases in verses 7-8 that speak to how God's Word makes us feel, or to the outcome it brings, which phrase do you need most in your life? **Circle this phrase and ask God to help see this through in your life.**

WEEK 3: DAY 6

Read the following devotion and answer the questions at the end.

"The Bible says that good things happen to good people."

"I know it says in the Bible that God hates the sin, but loves the sinner."

"The Bible says we need to be in the world, not of the world."

How many times have you heard someone say, "Well, the Bible says . . ." before saying something you really aren't sure the Bible says or not. All sorts of people, those who innocently mean well and those with agendas, twist the truth of the Bible. And if you don't know the Bible, they might end up twisting your vision of God, as well.

Read Acts 17:10-12, paying close attention to verse 11.

What does it say the Bereans did? The Bereans were praised because they took what they heard and compared it to the Word of God. They were looking to see if it matched up before they believed it. **What a great example for us to learn from.**

The next time someone, *anyone*, mentions something from the Bible that you aren't familiar with, you can take it at face value (and hope it's true and/or accurate), or you can go on a little hunt through Scripture making sure that what was said is actually true. Not only will this help you learn your Bible, but it will help you know exactly how to live your life.

- Why do we sometimes just accept what people say about God's Word without doing our homework?

  To take the easy way out.

- What do we risk when we don't compare everything to the truth of God's Word?

  It could twist our vision of God.

WEEK 3: DAY 7

REVIEW AND REFLECT

Did you learn anything this week that you didn't know going in? Did you discover something in God's Word that opened your eyes to something about God or His ways? Did you sense that there's more to the Bible than you thought? Have you come to understand how important God's Word is in your life? Take some time today and reflect on these things and the past seven days you've spent studying God's Word.

WEEK 3: WRAPPING UP

You've really gone deep in understanding the different aspects of hitting pause. You've studied the ins and outs of prayer. And you just finished a pretty intense focus on how and why to study God's Word. By now, you know what it means to *hit pause*, and why to do it. **But what is the point of mastering the art of hitting pause?**

What is the point of prayer? So you can see how super close you can be with God? What is the point of Bible study? To collect memory verses? To know Bible facts? No way. **The purpose of knowing God and studying His Word is so you can join Him in His mission to redeem the world.** You were never intended to keep your life to yourself. Knowing God means being used by God. We'll wrap up this book by focusing on what you can do to make your life count.

THE PAUSE EXTRA: #3

DO YOU STRUGGLE WITH MEMORIZING BIBLE VERSES?

Join the club. It's something that doesn't come easily for a lot of people. But, you're about to learn the absolute secret to memorizing a verse of Scripture. Seriously.

Here's a step-by-step method for memorizing a Bible verse.

Step 1: Choose Your Verse
Let's choose an easy one. If you already know this one, choose another one.

> I have hidden your word in my heart that I might not sin against you.—Psalm 119:11

Step 2: Read The Verse A Few Times
Read the verse silently two times. Then, read it out loud while still looking at the verse two times. Do this slowly, focusing on the words. Be sure to say the verse reference each time.

Step 3: Close Your Bible And Try Saying The Verse 10 Times Without Looking
If you have to look at first, that's cool. But by the last few times, you shouldn't have to look. This includes the verse reference, by the way.

Step 4: Without Looking, Write The Verse and Reference 10 Times
Use the space provided below to practice.

IT'S AS SIMPLE AS THAT! IF YOU'LL PUT THIS TO USE, YOU'LL BE SURPRISED HOW EFFECTIVE THIS METHOD IS. IT'S A GREAT WAY TO HIDE GOD'S WORD IN YOUR HEART!

WEEK 4: INTRO

If you recall in your study of *The Pause* with your group, you ended by talking about what hitting pause prepared you to do.

If you remember, you learned that hitting pause prepared you to live your life in play. Any of this ringing a bell yet?

When you studied *The Pause* with your group, you learned that hitting pause was like practicing for the big game, studying for a test, or learning your lines for a play. Hitting pause is preparation to shine in the big moment. Making time to seek God prepares you to live out your faith when the lights are shining brightly.

WHAT IS THIS BIG MOMENT YOU'RE PREPARING FOR?

Simple: your life.

This final week will help you see how knowing God and His ways will help prepare you for living a life of purpose. A life that has an amazing impact on people in the name of Christ.

Don't let up. Buckle down for this last week. You won't be sorry.

We are therefore Christ's ambassadors, as though God were making his appeal through us. We implore you on Christ's behalf: Be reconciled to God. —2 Corinthians 5:20

WEEK 4: DAY 1

Let's start the week by laying some groundwork. Read the following passages and follow the instructions.

YOU CAN HAVE ALL THE KNOWLEDGE OF GOD YOU WANT. BUT IF YOUR KNOWLEDGE OF GOD IS NOT BEING PRACTICALLY PUT TO USE THROUGH YOUR ACTIONS, THEN IT'S NOT BEING USED THE WAY GOD INTENDS. EXAMINE THE FOLLOWING VERSES TO SEE A GLIMPSE OF HOW THE BIBLE SPEAKS TO HOW YOUR RELATIONSHIP WITH GOD IS SUPPOSED TO MOVE YOU TO ACT.

Read 2 Timothy 4:1-2, paying close attention to verse 2.
In the space below, copy the phrase (or phrases) from the verse that most clearly speaks to you about being prepared to put your knowledge of God to use.

Preach the word, be instant...

Think about this:
- In your life, have you had "seasons" where you felt like you were in a better position to impact others for Christ? And maybe some seasons where didn't feel particularly useful? Why do you think this is?
- In your opinion, how does hitting pause help you prepare to be used by God?

- Yes, because of struggles in your own life that make you not pay attention ~~to God~~ to God.
- It gives you time to think.

59

Read 1 Peter 1:13.
In the space below, copy the phrase (or phrases) from the verse that speaks to you about being prepared to put your knowledge of God to use.

gird up the loins, be sober...

Think about this:
- Think about the world you live in each day. How can you apply Peter's phrase "prepare your minds for action" to your world? What does this action look like as a twenty-first century teenager?
- Think about how prepared your mind is for action on a day-to-day basis. Could you do better in this department? *Yes*

Read James 1:22-24.
In the space below, copy the phrase (or phrases) from the verse that speaks to you about how you're supposed to put your knowledge of God to use.

But ye be doers of the word and not hearers only.

Think about this:
- In your words, how is learning about God yet failing to put this knowledge into action deceiving yourself? *ONLY at church*
- How are you deceiving others, maybe even good friends of yours, by keeping to yourself the amazing difference a relationship with God can make in a person's life?

WEEK 4: DAY 2

Follow the instructions below to consider how you're impacting the world around you in Christ's name.

Hitting pause helps you grow closer to God. And growing closer to God helps you know more of His plan to save the world. On these pages, you'll see three categories. Follow the prompts to interact with each one.

FRIENDS AND ACQUAINTANCES

How are you living out your relationship with Christ in a way that makes Him more real to your friends and others?

YOUR
DAY-TO-DAY
ACTIONS

Write how your actions have recently demonstrated to others how awesome a relationship with God is. If you're feeling honest, list some recent examples of how your actions got in the way of sharing your devotion to God with others.

HELPING OUT
THOSE IN NEED

Part of knowing God is knowing His heart. And if you know even a little bit of God's heart, you know it breaks for those in need. What have you done lately for those who are needy?

WEEK 4: DAY 3

The Bible is full of examples of people who lived their faith in amazing ways. Here are three examples. In each of these stories, we see the evidence of these individuals putting their knowledge of God to use. Read the entire story or just the key verses, and interact with the questions that follow.

PERSON #1: PHILIP

Bio: Chosen by the apostles to help minister to the church in Jerusalem.

Context: Intense persecution had scattered the Jerusalem church. Philip had relocated north of Jerusalem to the region of Samaria.

The Whole Story: Acts 8:26-40
The Key Verses: Acts 8:34-35

THINK ABOUT THIS:

- Where is the proof in the story that Philip had spent time growing in His knowledge of God and of Scripture?

- How would Philip have missed this opportunity if he were not prepared to act on his faith?

PERSON #2: PAUL

Bio: A former enemy of the Church, Paul was radically and miraculously converted by God.

Context: Paul was traveling around the Mediterranean region on a missionary journey. In this story, he was in Athens, Greece.

The Whole Story: Acts 17:16-34

The Key Verses: Acts 17:16-21

THINK ABOUT THIS:

- Where is the proof in the story that Paul had spent time growing in His knowledge of God and of Scripture?

- How might this story have turned out differently if Paul was either unprepared, or unwilling to put His knowledge of God to work?

PERSON #3: PETER

Bio: Was leader of the disciples. Became leader of the Jerusalem church.

Context: Peter and the other disciples had been waiting in Jerusalem for the promised Holy Spirit. The Spirit suddenly came upon them during a feast called Pentecost. This is the first recorded sermon after Christ's death and resurrection.

The Whole Story: Acts 2:14-41

The Key Verses: Acts 2:40-41

THINK ABOUT THIS:

- Where is the proof in the story that Peter had spent time growing in his knowledge of God and of Scripture?

- What was the result of Peter's willingness to put his knowledge of God to work?

Read this quote. Then, take some time to reflect on it.

"ACTION IS THE PROPER FRUIT OF KNOWLEDGE."
—THOMAS FULLER

Thoughts to consider:

- What does this quote mean to you? What does it mean that action is the fruit of knowledge?

- What's the opposite of our knowledge leading to action?

- What's so wrong with our knowledge not leading to action?

- What happens to our action if there's no knowledge to drive it? In other words, if we don't make time to hit pause, how does it affect our ability to live godly lives and impact the world around us?

WEEK 4: DAY 5

Today you're going to practice an aspect of the pause.

Today, your only task is to focus on one person you know who really needs to have a relationship with Christ. Now here's the deal: You have a few ways of interacting with them as it pertains to what you've learned about hitting pause. You can pray for them now. You can commit to praying for them now and later. Or, if you're ready to see how hitting pause prepares you for a life of action, begin to engage this person in spiritual conversations.

The goal is to expose them to the love and grace of God in Christ. You can do this, because you've been hitting pause. You have been drawing closer to God. You have been preparing.

WEEK 4: DAY 6

Read the following devotion and answer the questions at the end.

We've now spent a great deal of time talking about how to live out of the knowledge you have of God. This entire week has challenged you to be a person whose relationship with God is the foundation of every aspect of your identity. You've been called to be a person who lives out their faith in a real way, in a way that impacts others.

The Apostle Paul got this concept. As we looked at on page 64, Paul was once an enemy of the Church. But God transformed Paul. The Bible tells us Paul went and regrouped for a few years. He had to take all his learning, all his knowledge of God, all his understanding of Scripture, and re-sort it all out. With the help of the Holy Spirit, Paul seemed to have figured it out, you know, since he is responsible for writing most of the New Testament.

But Paul figured out something else as well.

Read 1 Corinthians 9:19-24.

Here Paul is talking about how he figured out exactly how to use his knowledge of God. What Paul is saying here is that he carefully and compassionately crafted his message to fit the people to whom he was talking. From what we know about Paul, he could be a pretty gruff dude. Yet, in this passage we see him talking about how he tailored his story to meet the needs of the many different people he interacted with.

Paul's motivation for this approach seems to be an understanding that without God, people die. Out of love for others, Paul went to great lengths to make his story relevant.

- Are you motivated by compassion for those who do not know Christ? Does your concern for others help you overcome any fear you might have about talking about your faith?

- Do you miss opportunities to share your faith because you're unwilling to interact with people who might be different from you?

WEEK 4: DAY 7

REVIEW AND REFLECT

This is it. **You've basically come to the end.** As you go throughout your day, keep what you've learned over the last month in the forefront of your mind. Think about how you've grown closer to God. Think about how your actions have been motivated by this closeness. And identify how you'll use what you've learned to keep going deeper in your relationship with God. **It doesn't stop here, you know.**

REFLECT

WEEK 4: WRAPPING UP

There's a real problem that exists in the lives of Christ-followers. It affects both young people and adults. It's a real problem that has far-reaching results. The problem is that far too many people are totally OK with collecting knowledge about God, but not doing anything with it. Many Christ-followers go to church a few times a week. Read their Bibles every once in a while. Listen to Christian music and podcasts. And maybe even read Christian books like this one. But all the facts about God fail to make a difference in the way they think or live. **This is entirely unacceptable.**

Don't. Be. One. Of. These. People. When you live this way, you tell others who don't know God that He's really not worth getting to know. After all, you collect all this knowledge about Him and it doesn't change you one bit. When it comes to following Christ, this is not the picture the Bible paints. What's keeping you from being a real force for God? What is keeping you from learning about God and then putting your knowledge to action? Don't be OK with weak faith. **Be bold. Be brave. Be someone who makes a difference in God's name.**

HOW DO WE EVEN BEGIN TO TRY TO WRAP UP THIS JOURNEY YOU'VE BEEN ON THE LAST FEW WEEKS?

We could talk about how you feel, or some things you experienced. But the truth is that these things are fleeting. Your emotions are here one day, gone the next. And your experiences are hard to really build on. No, if we're going to wrap up this time it's best to do so by looking at a few truths . . .

TRUTHS BASED ON GOD, NOT ON US. TRUTHS THAT ARE BY NATURE UNCHANGING. TRUTHS YOU CAN BUILD ON.

When you think about what you've learned and how it has impacted you and will continue to impact you, start with these basic truths about God, His Word, and His ways.

Truth 1: God is knowable.

Don't let this pass you by. The God who made the world, the God who's all powerful and all knowing, this very God wants you to know Him. So, He made it so that you could.

Truth 2: Through prayer and reading the Bible, you can really and truly know God.

This should blow your mind. This should knock you off your feet. Not only is God knowable, but the key to knowing Him is not a secret! It's not a mystery! It's something you can do on your own. Amazing.

Truth 3: God's plan for reaching the world is you!

Well, more accurately, it's the Church. But you are the Church! Therefore, you're God's plan. And you're not plan B. You've always been His plan to take the hope and grace of Christ to the world. And that's super cool.

These truths form the foundation of all you have been learning over the past month. The challenge is for them to be part of the foundation of your life.

The worst thing you could do is leave this study unchanged. Don't be satisfied with staying the same.

MAKE TIME TO HIT PAUSE. Grow closer to God. And grow closer to God with the purpose of loving Him, being loved by Him, and showing His love to a needy world.

About the Author

Andy Blanks is the Co-founder and Publisher for youthministry360. Andy is passionate about God's Word and the transformation it brings in the lives of God's people. What brings Andy the greatest joy is seeing teenagers become sold-out disciples of Christ, following the Lord no matter the cost, and influencing the world around them in the name of Jesus. Andy is a writer, teacher, speaker, and a lifelong Boston Red Sox fan. He lives in Birmingham, AL with his wife, Brendt, and their three daughters.

All quotations taken from *THE COMPLETE GATHERED GOLD, A treasury of quotations for Christians*. John Blanchard, ed. Evangelical Press, 2006.

"Youth ministry, full circle." It's youthministry360's way of equipping and serving youth workers.

 At youth**ministry**360 we're bringing you an ever-expanding offering of BIBLE STUDY RESOURCES that are innovative, creative, and relevant.

 At youth**ministry**360, we're providing TRAINING for you by bringing to the table the voices of experienced youth ministers and youth ministry leaders.

 At youth**ministry**360 we're helping you connect to a COMMUNITY of other great youth workers through our social networks, special promotions, and events.

 At youth**ministry**360 we're using social media to help you NETWORK with other ministries in order to show you the best of what's out there.

youthministry360.com   1-888-96-ym360   Stay in touch

DNow
ONLINE

WANT SOMETHING FREE?
JUST FOR YOU?

We want to give you some free devotions just because we think you're awesome. No strings attached! To access your devotions, follow the steps below:

1. Scan the QR code below on your smartphone
2. OR, if you don't have a smartphone reader, just visit this
   URL: http://qrs.ly/du1930t

CONSIDER IT OUR WAY OF HELPING YOU GROW CLOSER TO GOD THROUGH KNOWING AND APPLYING HIS WORD.